Trust 'n Horses

A Guide to Successful
Trust-Based Horsemanship

The Collected Works
of
Franklin Levinson

Cover photo by Maria Victoria-Douka

ISBN-13: 978-0692142592
ISBN-10: 0692142592

Monday Creek Publishing
Ohio USA

Dedication

To my terrific, loving wife and life-partner Ilona Marianna Hargitai, my wonderful sister and brother-in-law Judy and Dennis Michaels and their 3 wonderful sons (Gary, Rob and Ken) for their life-long love and support, my wonderful mentors: David Kapralik (aka Iliili), Dr. Jerry Jampolsky and his wife Dr. Diane Cirincioni (authors and founders of Attitudinal Healing International), Dr. Lee Jampolsky (author, lecturer and great friend) and Dr. Jacob Liberman (author, lecturer and great friend).

For a horse there is only fear or trust. It either trusts it is safe or it is fearful it is not. Franklin Levinson

Foreword

Mutual trust is at the core of any successful, lasting relationship. Whether between humans or humans and another species such as a horse, dog or cat, the level of mutual trust dictates whether or not the relationship is functional, successful and will endure over time. I've often heard people say that their horse is acting mean, nasty, willful, stubborn and naughty. I always respond to those comments by saying that the horse is always innocent, and that judging a horse, as "being bad" by human standards is totally inappropriate. Yet many people expect horses to do as commanded. They also think the horse should respond the way they do to the world and think that undesirable equine behavior is something the animal is doing to them personally. Nothing could be farther from the truth. I hope that the concepts and philosophies expressed in this book help to promote a higher level of enjoyment and mutually successful experience between horses and their humans. Best wishes and good luck!

Franklin
www.trustnhorses.com

FRANKLIN AND HIS WIFE ILONA

Acknowledgments

I wish to extend much gratitude to: Carolyn Resnick, Carolyn Bourchier (UK), Shivam Kolhs, Steve Tomaino, Max Smith, Gail Murphy, Karen Fullbrook (UK), Pamela Gale (UK), Jenny Booth (UK), Wayne Rigg (Oz), Rob Armstrong (Oz), Elaine Hughes (Oz), Sylvia Steen (Greece), Vasilis Tourlakis (Greece), Marianna Gramatikakis (Greece), Mark Spanoudakis (Greece), Mark Mottershead (Horse Conscious, UK), Avril Tighe (UK), Karina Hawkridge (UK), Sharon Roper, Dave Dashner, Ron Tilden, Pellar Marion, Kip Mistral, Derek O'Byrne White (Ireland), Maggie Holley (Oz), Amanda Simpson & Stathis Katsarelias (Greece), Eva Fredrickson (Ireland), Rob Armstrong (Oz), Nasos Lolos (Greece), Lynne Hayes, Sue Hilgers, Elizabeth McCall, Jeff Wohler, Sheryl Brown, Jaclyn Fischer (Oz), Martha Grimes, Jojo Smith, Marina Marinopoulos (Greece), Shelley Burke, Anita Witt, Pat Martin, Barbara Rector, Sharon and Chris Cain, Kandio Voutsinou (Greece), Janice Meadowcroft, Francisco Palencia, and all the wonderful friends who have helped and supported me over the years and the many folks who have hosted my seminars in no less than seven countries around the world. *Thank you!*

Simple, clear, conscious requests are what the horse is looking for. Franklin Levinson

Contents

1 The Story of Pete 1

2 Learning to be With Horses...10

3 Rules of Engagement 23

4 Developing Trust with Equines (& Others).....................31

5 Five Tips for Getting That New Horse to Love You 40

6 Attitude is Everything with Horses and Humans 47

7 Conversation with Horses..56

8 Gaining Confidence with Horses.....................................65

9 Equine Facilitated Learning (EFL) 1 75

10 "We Hold These Truths to be Self-Evident..." 86

11 Quick Quote Reminders 94

12 Letters..106

About the Author..122

1 The Story of Pete

When I first was invited to Colorado to work on a ranch I kept hearing the other cowboys talk about an "outlaw" horse that was there. They were full of stories about how dangerous and aggressive he was: he couldn't be caught, wouldn't be loaded, reared and split his owner's head open, pulled back so hard when he was tied that he'd taken the shed with him, and dragged a guy who'd roped him all around a rocky field.

I heard the horse was going to be put down and sold for dog food because the owner didn't feel he was safe enough to sell to anybody. Since I know that a "mean

1

horse" is often just a very scared horse, I was anxious to see this animal. So I immediately headed out the corral for a look.

Way over in a corner of the corral, I saw a really cute quarter horse, and I could tell by the way he was acting - nervously looking around, swishing his tail, twitching his ears and wide eyed - that he was terrified of everything and anything. My heart went out to him and I wanted to give him a chance. So I asked his owner if I could work with him a bit.

The owner said, "I take no responsibility for what this horse does to you, how badly he hurts you or your hospital bills. Fine with me if you want to get yourself banged up. But don't say I didn't warn ya."

The next day, I got up early and went on down to the round corral they had Pete confined in. I didn't really have a specific plan for the horse. But I knew I needed to somehow gain his trust that he would be safe with me and that I would never hurt him.

The first thing I did was nothing. I simply observed the horse. I observed him for about two hours watching how his movements were: whether quick and nervous, lazy, agitated, anything I could notice. And also his overall attitude; like if he showed any interest in anything and would move towards it or if he jumped away from little things he perceived as scary like noises or shadows.

What I believed I saw in this horse was the most fear I had seen in any horse I had come across in my life. The slightest movement near him would send him running around the round corral looking for escape. Any little noise prompted the same reaction. My heart went out to this fearful animal. I felt so much compassion for him that my heart became a lump my throat.

What could have happened to this horse to make him so afraid? I could only imagine, and then I wanted to stop imagining it.

That first day I only stayed by the corral gate on the outside. I left the corral feeling thoughtful and yet excited at the possibilities of somehow turning this great fear I was seeing into great trust. I had worked with a lot of horses in my life, but none so fearful as this one.

The next day, I got up early and went down to the corral gate. Pete (actually his name at the time was Pistol Pete, but I did not like the reference to a gun) saw me and was actually looking at me with a tiny bit of curiosity. As is my way, I remained very quiet and calm and went inside the enclosure. I did not focus any attention on the horse other than a polite initial, verbal greeting. I never really looked at the horse's face or head at all.

My intention was to have a completely neutral presence. Just being quiet in a small area with a horse can maybe prompt some interest or, at least a little curiosity. I walked around the corral and just looked at different areas, without putting any attention to Pete. Well, this went on for about 20 minutes and darned if that horse didn't start to follow me around the corral. He kept what he thought was a safe distance, but he sure did come along. After a bit of time doing that, I began to praise him when I stopped by saying, "good boy."

The following day, Pete was actually at the gate waiting for me and it was then that I could see that he was going to make it. I continued on with what I had done the previous day and Pete got closer and closer as he followed me around the corral. Eventually he would walk right with me and be quite close, and he would stop and go when I did. I continued speaking to him in a calm and reassuring voice.

Towards the end of that second day, when Pete and I had stopped walking, I gave him a first little scratch on the withers and a "good boy." Just at that time Pete's owner happened to come by the corral to check things out. He saw this "outlaw" horse, which nobody could get near, standing about a foot to my right receiving quiet praise and a gentle scratch. And then he saw the horse following me around the corral, moving as I moved, changing directions and stopping when I did.

Well, the owner, who was a well-meaning fellow, said he couldn't believe his eyes. It was only a few days ago that he was considering putting Pete down because he was so dangerous to be near and he felt he would never be safe for anyone.

"Dang it! If that don't beat all! How'd you get that 'ol horse to do that?"

"Well, Sir," I said, "I just let him get used to me being around him without asking anything from him. I gave him bit of praise and space enough for him to not think I was going to try anything funny with him. I was patient and kind in my thoughts and actions. I knew he was just afraid and that all that dangerous behavior was the only way that he thought he could protect himself. He was like a little kid with a set of 6-shooters strapped to his hip. If you make him afraid he might just up and shoot you. So I made certain I did nothing that would make the horse think he needed to be afraid of me. If I had more time with him, I think he could turn out to be a pretty decent horse."

"Well, Franklin, I sure am liking what I have seen here with you and this horse. I never would have believed this horse would have settled down so fast with any human. Tell you what. I'll sell him to you for what he would have brought me if I had him put down at the killers."

So Pete became my horse and partner. He taught me even more about the importance of the roles of compassion and kindness, patience, calm and good leadership with horses. Pete took plenty of time to fully come around, but that was OK with me.

We still had our share of interesting challenges like when it came to trailer loading. I had managed to somehow load him up for the haul to the trailhead for a mountain ride. After the three-hour ride and we got back to the trailhead I could not get him back into the trailer. I had to ride him the three additional hours it took to get back to the ranch, most of it along a busy roadway. I decided then and there that he needed to go to trailer loading school. It took me four long, hard hours to get him to trust that the trailer wasn't going to swallow him whole and for him to walk in.

Now if he and I are near an open trailer door he wants to hop right in. Seems he has also developed a taste for adventure with me. We go off into the mountain wilderness together a lot. We have encountered bears, large herds of deer and elk and other wild animals. Pete - I now call him Sweet Pete - has never tried to dump me because he was so afraid of something or pull away from me out of fear. He may make a little jump if something startles him, but he never wants to leave my side. He watches my every move when I am anywhere he can see me. We share our emotions (horses are very empathetic) and we have a bond that will last all our lives.

These days Pete and I teach kids how to be kinder to animals and how to become a great leader for a horse in order to develop trust and respect with them. Because of the way I was able to help Pete, folks around the area began to ask me to help them with their problem horses. So 'Sweet Pete' and I have built a fine life together and we're still carrying our message of trust and love to as many people as we can.

2 Learning to be With Horses

Horses are like magnets for humans. People of all ages are drawn to the horse because of their beauty, grace, power, majestic stature and the mystery of their noble being. It's been that way throughout recorded history. In modern times, it has been clinically documented that just being around horses changes the brain wave patterns of humans, lowers blood pressure and reduces stress. We calm down and become more centered and focused in the present moment when we are merely around horses. We are transformed in a very positive way when in the presence of horses. It is no wonder that the beneficial effects of positive and appropriate interaction with horses should prove life enriching to grownups and children alike.

As I have been a professional horseman for nearly 50 years, I have known for a long time that horses can produce positive mental and emotional effects within the humans around them if the interaction was appropriate and mutually successful for both horse and human. Unfortunately, although many humans are attracted to horses, they often do not have any idea of how to approach and greet a horse safely. This stems from a lack of any solid knowledge about the horse itself. The only concept many humans have of horses is that people ride them. This sort of thinking objectifies the horse and put it in the category of a motorbike, carnival or circus ride. The horse is a sentient, thinking, feeling and relationship-based animal. It is naturally curious when it feels safe and wishes to make friends with those near it who show respect for it and communicate with it in an appropriate way.

Showing respect for a horse partially means not simply going into its personal space and touching it. We would not do this to another human and we do not wish a stranger to walk up to us and put their hands on us. Often people walk up to a horse and attempt to touch its face, nose or mouth. Sometimes they receive a bite on the finger for this rude indiscretion. Or, the horse might swing its rear at the human and try to kick them. These behaviors are not the horse being bad. The behavior is defensive and born out of fear that comes from another being not showing any respect for the animal's concerned reactions to the invasive behavior of the human. Horses communicate through body language. They evolved this way because, in the wild, if they make sound, they alert a predator to where they are. Thus, they are experts at body language communication. We humans are not and mostly are unaware of our own body language and the messages we convey unconsciously to others via how we move, or simply just sit or stand. The horse most often has tried to tell the human approaching it that it is not happy with what the human is doing. But, we move forward unconsciously with our agenda and we either miss the animal's communication entirely or we ignore it. Then, when we get kicked or bitten because we did not pay attention to what the horse was trying to tell us, we judge the animal as bad. When we judge an individual as bad, we can then tend to think that punishment is called for. No matter what the behavior of a horse or how dangerous it is, it is always innocent and never, ever deserves to be punished. I have seen horrible abuses heaped upon horses by ignorant humans seeking to punish this innocent animal who was merely acting out of fear for its own survival. There are appropriate consequences for unwanted behavior that teach rather than punish.

I had a ranch on the Hawaiian island of Maui for 30 years. Many years ago at that ranch I began The Maui Horse Whisperer Experience, which was an experiential, interactive, hands-on experience of horses for non-horse people. Of course horse owners were invited as well. The positive effects of the successful inter-species communication were immediate and, sometimes, life altering. The confidence and self-esteem of individuals who were able to bond and communicate successfully with the horses dramatically improved and the improvement was immediate. People would drop their projections, misconceptions and judgments about the horse, and themselves, once the communication became conscious, appropriate, and mutually successful.

For children with mental and emotional disorders the positive benefits of the experience with the horses was frequently profound. Children with Attention Deficit Disorder (ADD and ADHD) would magically focus on the horse for long periods of time when either grooming or leading the horses. Once they understood how to ask for and receive cooperation from the horse, their self-esteem went sky high. What a wonderful sight it is when I see a shy, withdrawn, fearful child standing tall and confident as they lead a 1200-pound animal through an obstacle course of a series of twists, turns and stops.

Children with Autism who would come to me mostly withdrawn and very much in their own world, would begin to say new words and attempt to express themselves as rarely seen by their parents and therapists. Given the lead rope of an appropriate horse they would proudly lead the horse around the ranch for extended periods of time and not want to give them up. Observers would stand there with mouths wide open and tears streaming down their faces to see such profound and wonderful responses in their children and wards. Once again, the horse is easily recognized as a positive force and influence for humans. Prisons in the US have instituted programs to assist in the rehabilitation of inmates by teaching them how to train wild horses. Untrained horses from the open ranges of several states are given over to some prisons so the prisoners can train and gentle these horses to get them ready to be adopted out. Techniques are shown the prisoners on how to gently communicate with a fearful horse and develop the trust needed to help the horse accept human contact and interaction. The inmates discover that respect, gentleness, mindfulness, compassion and kindness go a lot farther than brutality, dominance and force. These programs are so successful as to have become the single most effective form of rehabilitation for the penal system in America today.

At about the same time The Maui Horse Whisperer Experience came about, I began the 'Leading with Quiet Strength' program. This is a leadership/teambuilding program developed for corporations seeking to advance the leadership qualities and skills of top executives. There are now a numerous programs across the country that focus on these goals for the corporate world utilizing guided, successful interaction with horses. In this age of corporate greed, poor management, distrust, and wide spread fraud, a program that teaches responsibility, accountability, respect, trust and mindful interaction via success with horses, was a natural development for me. 'Enlightened leadership' is a goal being pursued by many top organizations and even some governments, around the world. Accountability and responsibility are taught through the quality of the interaction with the horses and the feedback is immediate. The success or failure of the interaction and communication is tossed back into the face of the human right away by the response of the horse. If there is a problem, it can be quickly recognized and corrected by the human through a change in attitude and/or behavior. Once everything is back on track, the interaction again becomes successful. A horse forgives us our mistakes. If a horse is abused by a human and eventually the human changes their way of dealing with the horse, the horse will forgive the human their mistakes and accept the friendship if it is offered sincerely and appropriately.

The principles of mutually successful interaction with horses are basic and easy to understand. The horse is the perfect mirror of the human that is with it (horses do not lie). The horse is looking to have feelings of safety and peace always. This is because the horse is a 'prey' animal always looking over its shoulder for the 'predator'. If the human is trying to control the animal for whatever reason, this produces fear within the horse. If the human is unconscious around the horse, this makes the horse fearful as well. If the human is disrespectful of the horse (inappropriate touching, movements, sounds, thoughts or feelings), this produces fear with the horse too. When the human begins to make conscious, thoughtful movement and appropriate requests, rather than demands of the horse, cooperation begins to happen. When a human waits for and notices the responses of the horse to the human's communications, that is showing acknowledgement and respect for the horse. Trust and respect are earned with horses in much the same way as with people, with the added aspect of great guidance and leadership coming forward from the human. It is the human's responsibility to approach the horse as a great parent approaches a child. Along with the love, compassion, patience and consistency of a great parent, comes confident, skillful, knowledgeable guidance and leadership. In the wild, the horse gets its sense of peace and safety from the herd leader. Unfortunately for the domesticated horse, there usually is no great human leader filling that role of the herd leader. Relationships between domesticated horses are somewhat confusing and difficult for the horses, as stables and barns are an un-natural environment for horses. There are few humans making appropriate requests that the horse can easily understand and comply with. Horses miss this good leadership. What is often the case, are humans making unconscious, inappropriate demands, trying to control this big beast through dominance, punishment and restraint and abusing the animal through ignorance and misconception. Compliance is frequently done through bribing with food or inducing fear. A child, even one with mental or emotional disorders, given a little insight into joining appropriately with a horse, becomes the natural leader the horse is looking for. Peace abounds, and cooperation and compliance come forth from the horse when the communication from the human is kind and appropriate. Actually, children can become successful with a horse quicker and easier than many adults. This is because children are frequently less judgmental, less controlling and more open to 'heart to heart' forms of communication than many adults.

Simple, clear, conscious requests are what the horse is looking for. Stop, go, backup and turn this way or that, are examples of simple requests that a human can make of a horse, clearly and consciously. When the horse complies, a 'thank you' in the form of a total release of pressure of the request (stop asking for anything and offer the animal a few moments of peace) is all that is needed. Horses understand the acknowledgement of being shown simple respect. They know that they are being thanked and acknowledged when peace and a little praise is offered. I am not talking about fawning over a horse because it is compliant. Overdone praise becomes shallow and meaningless. A simple "Good Boy (or Girl)" and a short quiet time, is all that is required. There is a balance to be struck. We humans seem to have a tendency to either over do or under do something. Being out of balance has become our way of being in this modern, technologically based world. Many of us seem to be missing out on any sort of experience of our 'natural' world. There is a natural balance to a horse's being. There is to ours as well, but we do not see or feel it because of our need to 'control'. This puts us out of balance a lot in our lives. We are either too much or too little. Or, at least it seems that way. Appropriate, successful interaction with horses can lead us back to that natural balance because to be successful with a horse that natural balance must be present in the communication. A natural balance begins to appear when there is consideration, thoughtfulness, awareness and kindness present in the interaction. 'Balance' is another of life's great lessons and attributes that can be learned through mutually successful interaction with horses and experiences of nature.

The benefits of this type of simple, yet successful interaction with horses, is immediate, profound and wide reaching. It is part of my personal mission, and that of my wife and partner Ilona Staikou Hargitai, to bring these incredibly beneficial aspects of being with horses to the forefront of our association and programs at the new Silvaland Equestrian and Life Enrichment Center soon to open on Corfu.

Trust and respect are earned with horses in much the same way as with people, with the added aspect of great guidance and leadership coming forward from the human. Franklin Levinson

3 Rules of Engagement

When we think of the term 'rules of engagement' we might possibly think of warfare. In years gone by, officers would actually sit down with their enemies and formalize the terms of their battles. They would decide on acceptable weapons, locations, dealing with wounded and more. It seems to me that the British were often known for doing this. I think it occasionally worked until modern warfare took staging war from the hands of so-called 'officer gentlemen' and placed it into the hands thugs, zealot mass murderers and people who had little to no sense of compassion or fair-ness. I am thinking of a totally different reference for 'Rules of Engagement.'

Successful, efficient, yet gentle horse training has its own, special set of 'rules of engagement.' It is the engagement of the horse's mind that I am referring to. Many humans do not realize how important it is to effectively engage the horse's mind during training and how to do that. Actually effective horse training is all about engaging the horse's mind. Many humans think horses have such a limited attention span that they overlook whether or not they have actually connected with the horse's mind during their sessions. Some folks think the horse is so stupid that their minds can only be engaged for a very short period of time. They think that if an hour has gone by that their horse has been taxed mentally to its limit. This is an erroneous and unfair judgment of the horse's mental capacities and capabilities.

Horses are very smart actually and have the ability to learn things quickly and lastingly. Abuse a horse just one time and they can immediately learn how to avoid that abuse in the future and perhaps the person who abused them as well. If a human makes a horse fearful that horse will immediately learn to avoid the source of the fear.

Feelings of safety are the most important feelings a horse can have. Being a prey animal (eaten by various predators), trusting it is safe in the moment allows the horse to have a fuller life. That trusting that it is safe, gives the horse the confidence to eat, drink and sleep. It is the leader(s) of the herd and their effective leadership and guidance that give the other members of the herd that confidence and those feelings of safety (safety exists only as a feeling and is not part of the 'outside' world).

To do this they actively engage the other members of the herd. They engage the minds of these other horses through their guidance of the direction, speed and actions of the herd. Additionally, their body language (posturing), the sounds they make, as well as passing information to the herd through non-physical means (empathetic, which is shared emotion and telepathic, which is shared mental images) cues the other herd members to respond. We humans need to develop our methods and rules of engagement to effectively communicate our wishes and desires to our horses. We need to become the great herd leaders for our horses. It is not solely about being 'alpha' or dominant. There must be 'appropriateness' to the communication.

Some of these Rules of Engagement should be: Knowing exactly what you want the horse to do before you ask. Having a clear mental image of the action you want the horse to perform is extremely important to have successful interaction with your horse. These things help your requests to be clear for the horse. If you confuse a horse by not being precise in your desires and requests, don't expect the horse to be able to understand and be able to try to do as asked. Having a very good understanding of when a horse is trying to comply with a request, and then, when and how to reward that animal's effort is also vital to the success of the training. Rewarding a horse for it's trying to comply with a request should come immediately when the horse makes a good effort. A suitable and appropriate reward is a brief rest and break from the pressure of the request. Accompanied by a bit of praise like a "Good boy," a short rest is all that is required for a horse to know it is being rewarded for its effort. Additionally, understanding how much 'pressure' to put into a request is vital. Being 'over the top' with pressure produces fear in the horse and, therefore, resistance. Not having enough pressure in a request prompts the horse to ignore the request or not take the request seriously enough to try.

A few additional Rules of Engagement could be: Clarity in the human's mind helps create clarity in the mind of the horse. If we confuse a horse, we make it afraid. If we frustrate a horse, that makes it fearful as well. If we blame a horse and judge it as bad because it makes a mistake or 'acts out' (unwanted behavior because we have produced fear within the horse), this makes any situation with a horse worse. If we get angry at our horses and take their behavior(s) personally, this makes us tend to want to punish them. Punishment should never be an option. Neither should a human ever take a horse's behavior personally. It is never doing anything to us. It is just being a horse. Reprimands and providing consequences for unwanted behavior is very acceptable as it sets up a learning situation for the horse and helps the horse understand it can take responsibility for the outcomes of its behavior. Through the practical application of these 'rules' we can become more effective leaders for our horses and have more successful training happen for our horses. With horses, appropriate reprimands and consequences can be in the form of movement. Any movement is work for a horse. Horses are naturally lazy, preferring to move about as peacefully as possible. This is not a bad thing as it needs to conserve energy so it has enough to run from a predator when need be. Physical or mental abuse should never an option.

Take every problem that arises with a horse as an opportunity to teach something. Teaching the horse it can trust the human is the most important lesson it can learn. This is accomplished through the human's ability to be skillful, patient, precise and, most of all, kind and compassionate.

I think earning the trust of the horse, helps us to trust ourselves. By being trust worthy for our horses, we learn more about the nature of trust and how to trust. Franklin Levinson

4 Developing Trust with Equines (& Others)

I love the subject of trust. It's trust that allows humans, as well as horses, to have full, rich lives. Without the feeling of trust, we are always looking over our shoulder, as the horse is always looking over its shoulder for the predator. There is another word that is related to the nature of trust and that is "feeling". Where do trust, safety, security and peace really exist? They exist in feelings. Are we safe when riding in a car? It seems to me, we are only as safe as we think we are. We can only have 'feelings' of safety. So, it might be said that trust and safety do not really exist outside us. It is an internal process and really does not exist in the world beyond our consciousness.

My childhood was anything but peaceful or filled with feelings of trust. My Dad was a rage-acholic. He was very unstable emotionally. When children are not given the support of a consistently emotionally calm parent, it is hard for them to have feelings of trust and safety. It was hard for me as a child, never having feelings that everything was really okay. Fortunately, my Dad was into horses, Polo to be more accurate. He liked the exercise he got from riding and the glory and prestige that came from playing 'the sport of kings'. For me it opened up a world where trust and safety did exist within the relationships I was able to establish with our horses. From a very young age, horses would calm down when they were close to me. There was something about me that attracted them to me in a very gentle way. I didn't understand what it was that helped them feel that they could trust that they were safe when they were with me. Perhaps, it had something to do with the fact that I had no agenda when I was with them other than to have an enjoyable experience no matter what we were going to do, even something as energetic and hard work as playing polo. If my horse ran over the ball or made some sort of mistake on the field, there was no punishment dished out, as I saw other players do.

Mistakes happen, they do not deserve punishment, but rather, be taken as opportunities to learn and mature.

Feelings of trust happen for children and horses the same way, from appropriate guidance and support. In the case of children that usually comes from the parents. In the case of horses, that comes from the mature horses and the leader(s) of the herd. For the domesticated horse, it is supposed to come from the humans who have the responsibility of caring for the horse. I instinctively knew these were important for the horse, even though I still wasn't aware of how important they were to me. Magically, when I could tell the horse felt safe and calm with me, I felt that same sense of safety and peace too. It seems to me that in order to give a horse a sense of safety and peace we have to find it within ourselves first. I have found this to be especially true when working with troubled teens that come to my ranch. Part of what I ask them to do is to help the horse feel safe with them, to trust that the human will not abuse them and will protect them. When they help the horse to feel safe and calm, they feel safer and calmer themselves. I think earning the trust of the horse, helps us to trust ourselves. By being trust worthy for our horses, we learn more about the nature of trust and how to trust. Trusting ourselves, to me, is related to having faith in one's self, which translates to self-esteem and confidence.

I believe horses are attracted to peace. Because it is a prey animal, always weary of the possibility of a predator nearby, it knows terror. Terror is the feeling of being helpless to save our lives in the presence of mortal danger. Since the events of 9-11 we all are more familiar with feelings of terror. Perhaps we can have more compassion now for prey animals, such as horses, when they respond out of fear. Most of the so-called, 'bad behavior, of horses, is them responding fearfully to something happening in the moment. It is not out of some premeditated or stubborn desire to go against our wishes. I look at the flight response of horses as moving to peace, rather than running from fear. They want that safe, peaceful feeling again, desperately. When our goal with the horse is to become a peace bringer above anything else, we establish a sense of trust in the horse that is so profound they will do most anything they are capable of that we request of them, even something that may seem life threatening (such as jumping through a hoop of fire). A horse that does not trust does not feel safe. Just as with a paranoid human, a fearful horse will never be fully present or able to respond appropriately in the moment. 'Trust' is a key to success in almost any situation for the horse or the human.

Even with all my antennas up and functioning well, my intuition finely tuned and my inner voices loud and clear things happen that I would have rather they had not. I certainly cannot control anything except for one thing, my own thoughts. The only thing I can ever expect to 'change' is myself. I can't control the weather, the thoughts of another or what they do. I can't change my family or anybody. It is only my own thoughts that I can really exert any type of 'control' or authority over. I can change my mind, but not yours. I can influence you only by what I do, which is reflective of how I think. If I live my life from a trusting, loving place and you experience that paradigm through me, you may find it attractive enough to want to experience that trust (peace) more in your own life.

Horses are totally honest. They never lie. They are incapable of it. If a horse exhibits behavior that looks like aggression, it's really honest fear. If they look sick, they are. There are many ways to mask a horse's ill health to make them look OK. Given the absence of a 'mask' (often a drug) of some sort, a horse is very forthcoming with how it is feeling physically and emotionally. I think they are more forthright than we are, as they are not concerned with their 'image'. Also, we can be feeling not so good and still function, do our jobs and have a decent day. So can the horse. If you know how to listen to the horse, they will always tell you the truth about how they are feeling and, often, still be ready to do their job.

In the programs I present, *Training Through Trust* and *Life Enrichment Through Success with Horses*, I really emphasize the importance of trust for the horse. Safety equals trust, which means peace for the horse. It's the same for humans too. Who doesn't want to be able to have a sense of safety in their life? We all need to trust in something, and that trust begins with ourselves, with our connection to each other and nature. We are not separate beings, alone and autonomous, as our ego would have us think. As that horse who finds himself alone, way in the back of the herd, is more vulnerable to being eaten by a predator, so are we more vulnerable to doubt and fear by keeping ourselves separate from each other.

I didn't start to trust myself until later in my life. Not getting the proper support and love as a child prompted me not to trust that I was lovable, or OK, or even worthy of love. I learned not to trust humans. However, I did learn to trust horses early on. They did not hide their fear in order to look brave. They did not need to appear any other way than how they really were. This is probably because there is not the same kind of self-serving ego in the horse that exists in humans. Now that I am older and have spent most of my life with horses, I have come to trust them even more. I have learned how to receive their communications better (they are fluent communicators) and respond appropriately. Horses trust me and do it quickly, because I have dropped any agenda other than being truly helpful for the horse. By becoming a peace bringer for the horse, they are attracted to me. They move to me, without hesitation. They show me immediate trust and the utmost respect. I earn it though. I earn their respect by being the respectful herd leader for them; I earn their trust by being the trustworthy parent. They are peaceful with me, because I have become more peaceful within myself.

A good friend of mine, the late Dr. Wayne W. Dyer, renowned author and lecturer, wrote about St. Francis of Assisi in a recent book. When he visited my ranch recently we talked about what made St. Francis so attractive to animals. It was trust. The animals trusted him so very much and looked to him as the 'great parent' or the 'great father', which he was for them. Their trust was immediate and unwavering because he spoke only of peace and kindness to the animals and only had that as his intention for them. Perhaps we can take these lessons of peace for the animals into our lives as well. Then we can help each other to 'trust' more too. Maybe we can find ways to become peace bringers to each other, to have the intention to be kind and truly helpful. Perhaps then, we'll be able to trust each other more also. Earning a horse's trust may be just the practice we need. Earning the trust of the animals in our care brings an abundance of rewards to us as well as to the animals. Trust = Safety = Peace.

5 Five Tips for Getting That New Horse to Love You

People oftentimes start out on the wrong foot with a new horse, which quickly escalates into a major battle that the horse usually wins by employing scare and evasion tactics. Here is a brief discussion on this topic and five or more ways you can bond with your new animal so he "runs to greet you, rather than away from you"?

When I greet a horse for the first time, any horse of any age, gender or stage of training, I connect from a polite distance before I get within the horse's 'personal space' or range. I direct some 'thoughtful, kind' energy towards the horse verbally and with my body language (I don't square off to the horse, I let him experience my side or profile). I make certain I am centered and focused and that my breathing is relaxed. I endeavor to be in a calm but very aware state of mind. Horses greet us consciously and expect us to do the same. Also, a degree of confidence within the human helps the horse begin to feel confident about the human. As feelings of safety and peace are so very important to a prey animal like the horse, it is important to try to help the animal maintain those positive feelings. My only agenda is for the horse to feel safe and confident that it will be safe with me.

Beginning a relationship with a new horse is a lot like beginning a new relationship with a human. A few basic ingredients will help to insure a positive experience for all. First of all, show courtesy, respect, thoughtfulness and kindness. Do not enter the horse's personal space unless invited to by the horse's welcoming attitude. Don't put your hand on the horse's face or crowd his head. Stand by his shoulder as to not make him feel any more claustrophobic than he already naturally is. Speak in a soothing and confident tone. Keep your hands down. It's thoughtful and respectful to learn something about his language before you attempt to communicate with him.

Gain an understanding that the horse wants to connect with you and how to do it. Don't just wing it. Do a bit of homework first; read up on horses or watch an educational film. It will help you and the horse to understand and feel good about each other easier and faster. Once invited to come closer to the horse by its attitude and body language, do so but only for a few seconds and then retreat or back away from the horse. Wait a bit and then go closer, after a few moments and maybe a little scratching gently on the horse's shoulder, back away again. You will see the horse begin to watch you as you move back and forth and follow you intently with his gaze and head. This advance and retreat behavior you do around the horse actually helps the horse feel safer with you and rather curious about you at the same time. It is very unpredator like. Horses like that.

Frequently humans over-input a horse even though we think we are just showing affection. Think about how horses greet each other in the wild. They share breath and then generally give each other some room. Horses being affectionate scratch each other with their teeth usually for only a short period of time. I have seen humans endlessly patting, rubbing and scratching a horse and the horse is actually leaning away from the human and would move away if it could (usually the horse is tied), but the human ignores the horse's response to the constant touching and keeps it up. Humans are usually very thoughtful about how they touch another human's body, but not so when touching a horse's body. They just do it and usually right on the horse's nose (a very sensitive and private body part). You never see horse's scratching each other's noses. Sometime a horse will love to be scratched for quite a long while or touched a certain way for an extended period of time, but we humans need to be sensitive to the horse's responses just like we are with each other and wait to be invited to extend physical contact and then pay attention to the response of the animal as to whether or not our touch is appreciated.

I met my Colorado horse, "Sweet Pete", when his name was "Pistol Pete". I was told the horse was uncatchable, couldn't be ridden safely without rearing, unloadable, dangerous, vicious, not to be trusted and, as one person who saw the horse hurt another person put it, "was a candidate for the firing squad". When I heard that, I couldn't wait to meet him. What I saw was one of the most fearful animals I had ever seen. He was 9 years old, beautiful, but so full of fear of humans he couldn't get far enough away, fast enough. Someone must have really hurt him badly over time. Anyway, I got him herded into a round pen where I promised him I would not approach him unless he invited me to or he came to me first. I sat down in the center of the ring and waited. Sometimes I walked around, I talked to him a lot, always reassuringly. I never squared my body to him. I sat again for a while and then I walked for a while. Sometimes I moved around him, never right at him. I wanted him to feel free with me, and that doing anything I wanted had to be his desire also. I continued this process for two days. At the end of the second day, Pete was following me around. He just started doing it, I never asked him to. I never pushed him around the round pen. Eventually, he invited me to touch him, which I did on the shoulder and briefly. We had begun our relationship in earnest. When we got to the trailer loading sessions, he gave me the longest trailer loading session I have ever had, four hours before he got in. Now he leaps into the trailer when I point to it. When he is with me at a program I am presenting he is loose by my side all the time. He'll go and stand somewhere if I ask him, but he rather stay right by my side. He finds me, he catches me, he is free to make this choice himself and he does. If you do your homework first, then show respect to the horse, kindness, compassion, thoughtfulness and the leadership of a great parent, you will be rewarded with one of the greatest relationships that exist in Nature.

So what are the five things to get any horse to love you quickly (besides apples and carrots)? They are:

(1) Compassion (2) Kindness (3) Respect (4) Patience (5) Great Leadership.

6 Attitude is Everything with Horses and Humans

I receive a daily inspirational message from a good friend who is an author on spiritual topics and a motivational speaker named Alan Cohen. The quote for today is; "We see the world not as it is, but as we are." The particular author of this quote is marked as 'unknown'. I think what it says is so true of our lives in general. Our lives are how we think they are and how we think is how we are. If our attitude is one of 'how much can I get' or 'what can I take from this situation' or 'I am not getting enough', we see our lives as somehow limited and we are never to be fulfilled. This is an indication of a belief that we are somehow 'lacking' and never having or being enough. Seeing the world thru the eyes of 'lack' leaves us feeling frustrated and incomplete.

Relating this 'attitude is everything' theory to training and communicating with horses produces immediate results of success or failure. First off, if we think horses do not understand us or do not have the cognitive skills for two-way communication with a human, then we will never have that sort of connection with any horse. If we think it is a possibility then with some coaching or training, it can become a reality. As the horse is a prey animal, which means other animals eat it, it has big antennas that are constantly scanning its environment for predators. For a horse there is only fear or trust. It either trusts it is safe or it is fearful it is not. Once this is truly understood about horses, it becomes obvious that if a human can help a horse to feel safe and trust it is safe, then the horse will accept the human as its 'herd' leader just as it does the herd leader in the wild. I have become a successful communicator with horses because I have as my 'attitude' that I want to become a peace bringer to the horse first and foremost. I have come to understand that if I can promote feelings of peace and safety within a horse, I become like a magnet for them, attracting them to me. Once they experience feelings of peace and safety (i.e. 'trust') they just want to stay around where these feelings originate (with me). This is the key to all bonding, connection and successful communication with horses and humans as well. Feelings of safety are more important to the horse than food, water or shelter. The horse's sense of safety (survival) is first and foremost in it's mind. If it is feeling safe and peaceful it is not worried about survival and it can focus what is happening in its environment and whatever is being requested of it without fearful thoughts entering its mind and distracting it. When we humans have an attitude of fear or paranoia, it can distract us so much that we become dysfunctional. Imagine what it might be to always be fearful of being killed. That is what can happen for a horse that is never supported in, or able to find those all-important feelings of peace, trust and safety.

Peace, trust and safety, do not exist in the outside, physical world. They are internal feelings within all of us. We either feel them or we don't. It is the same for the horse. It feels safe and trusts that it will be safe or it does not. Resistance from a horse is most often brought on by fearful feelings. Every time you hear someone say a horse is stubborn, willful, bad, mean, vicious or any other negative thing, it is an improper projection of the human's attitude on to the horse and an inaccurate interpretation of the horse's actions. For the horse's behavior is only a symptom of fear. It is like a child who is fearful and acting out (being stubborn, willful or some such negative behavior) because of its fearful feelings about something new, unknown or scary.

Attitudes are hard things for humans to change. We are so attached to our points of view and opinions that, in some cases, we are willing to die for them. I can certainly understand being willing to die for a cause that would be considered morally 'just'. Although many so called 'just causes' don't seem to be more than personal preferences. To change our attitude about something frequently takes some sort of catastrophic occurrence in our lives. For instance, a near death experience or a major illness can change our attitudes about life and how we live it very fast. Isn't it a shame that we have to experience some sort of trauma in order for humans to prioritize 'gratitude' into our consciousness of everyday feelings? Wouldn't it be interesting to see what would occur between people if an attitude of tolerance was developed towards those who we view as different from us? Imagine how our lives might be altered for the better and the lives of all those we encounter and interact with be changed, if we cultivated attitudes of a positive nature instead of negative thought patterns. It is my feeling that an attitude of fear is being permeating around this country and the world. I have chosen not to succumb to this mass consciousness of fear. I do not want to be always looking over my shoulder for the predator. The only way I can achieve feelings of inner peace for myself is to endeavor to remember my own sense of peace and not buy into the fearful attitudes and thoughts that seem to abound around me. I can take responsibility for my own sense of well-being and happiness by keeping an 'attitude of gratitude' about the blessings in my life and not dwelling on what I think is wrong. I can help things I would change in my life by knowing I am giving my best effort to all situations and endeavors. I practice being my best through bringing my best to the horses whenever I interact with them. If the interaction is successful for both the horse and me, then I have immediate feedback that I have, in fact, brought my best forward.

Horses will not eat, sleep, drink or anything else if they are in a fearful emotional state. They can only run to find that safe place again. They proactively seek feelings of peace and safety by running in a direction that their leader guides them to. Once a place of safety is 'felt' they stop running and return the normal routine of eating, playing and sleeping. Many humans see a horse's fearful feelings and the reactions they cause, as the horse being 'bad'. We judge horses and humans inappropriately all the time. We project our judgmental attitudes on all around us. We seek to make others wrong and bad so our egos can feel superior and good. We make horses bad and wrong so we have an excuse to place responsibility somewhere other than ourselves. This also gives us an excuse to punish, control and dominate another being. This makes many humans feel superior. How sad a commentary it is on the human condition that we innately feel so small and inferior that we have to hurt an innocent animal or others in order for us to ultimately feel good about ourselves or, to not take responsibility for the outcomes of our unsuccessful and inappropriate ways of communicating and dealing with any relationship.

I propose a moratorium on negative attitudes and judgments. I suggest seeking a successful outcome for all through the extension of compassion, kindness and tolerance. To be successful with horses also requires skillful leadership. Perhaps negative attitudes could change without a catastrophe happening first simply because we desire to have better, more fulfilling lives. We could choose to be thankful for what is and work to improve what is not. We could choose peace over conflict if we are willing to suspend judgment. So, I do think attitude is everything as it relates to horses and humans. How you think something is, is how it is for you. Your children, spouse, career, your horse and your life are what you think they are. Now what do you think about that?

If we are not able or unwilling to read and correctly interpret a horse's body language, we may as well be speaking a foreign language to each other. Franklin Levinson

7 Conversation with Horses

During a recent horsemanship/horse training seminar I was providing with my wife and co-presenter Ilona Staikou Hargitai, a thought came to me that I felt shed additional light on how to become even more successful with horses. Exploring the concept that working with horses is like having a successful conversation with them, made a lot of sense to me. The online Cambridge Dictionary defines a conversation this way: "(a) talk between two or more people in which thoughts, feelings and ideas are expressed, questions are asked and answered, or news and information are exchanged."

Additionally, I think for the conversation to be successful it has to be mutually successful. We have all had a one-sided conversation where whoever we are speaking with is not paying attention, distracted or trying to control the flow of energy and information. These sorts of experiences can leave us feeling dissatisfied, incomplete, angry and disrespected among many other negative feelings. Imagine what it might be for a horse to have mostly one-sided conversations with humans because even many well-intentioned humans do not understand how to have a conversation with a horse.

Many humans simply do not understand the mind, psychology, language and behavioral tendencies of horses. They feel that they must dominate and control the animal to get what they want from it. This is indeed a sad state of affairs for the horse. Horses always want to communicate with whoever is near them. They are a very social animal and desire to have relationships with those around them. We humans often only show up as the caretaker and boss for our horses. When the boss speaks, it is always a one-sided conversation. Not being heard within a conversation goes along with not being respected. If the person we are having the conversation with doesn't listen to what we are saying or even try to understand our point of view, it creates frustration, resentment, a collapse of communication, and destroys the possibility of a good relationship.

If we take a hard look at the failure of our relationships with our horses, I think we would find that our inability to have a simple, successful conversation with them is partially at the core of the problem. We simply do not know how to listen to them and respond appropriately. Nor do we have the desire to do so much of the time, as we want what we want from them, and we want it now. We tend to think we need to show up as the boss of the horse rather than a respectful friend and trusted leader. I am not suggesting that our conversations with our equine friends be all sugar-coated and honey sweet. This would not be honest or reasonable, as some conversations need to contain information about rules, boundaries, procedures and the like. This is serious information that needs to be received in a positive way to be effective and helpful. Both parties having the conversation need to be open and respectfully giving and receiving information.

Being a good conversationalist is somewhat of an art I think. Whether it is between humans or humans and horses, the same elements need to be present for the exchange to be considered mutually successful. The first important element might be a common language. After all, if one person only speaks French and the other only Greek, great success would seem to be difficult to achieve. For horses, their main mode of communication is body language. If we are not able or unwilling to read and correctly interpret a horse's body language, we may as well be speaking a foreign language to each other. A successful conversation also has an element of mutual respect within it. If we determine someone is not listening to us, they are showing disrespect. We can feel it and so can the horse when we are not listening to it or paying attention. The conversation quickly becomes an unpleasant and a frustrating experience when this is the case. This one main point is at the root of many problems humans have with their horses. We are not listening to our horses and making a sincere effort to understand what they are trying to say. Mostly, a horse is attempting to communicate its fearful feelings or its feelings of safety. We so often seem to ignore their efforts at communication.

My strongest belief is that all behavior we do not want from our horses comes from the animal trying to communicate that it is afraid. If the horse shows resistance to a request (or demand), we tend to judge it as being stubborn and bad. We then tend to shout at the horse or use force and punishment to make it comply with what we want. At that point, the mutually successful conversation goes out the window. An alternative to this unsuccessful conversation might be to first be very clear and precise with what we wish to communicate. The more precise and accurate we can be in our communications, the better chance we have of being understood. Not knowing what we want to say makes it very difficult to say it. Horses do not suffer from this inability to be clear and precise with communications as we human can tend to do. Additionally, the horse is not trying to manipulate us the way we do with it. What the horse is telling us all the time is how it feels in any given moment. But we tend to ignore the horse's conversation in deference to our own agenda.

Here is a simple example of beginning a conversation between a human and a horse. First, we want to calm ourselves and focus in the present on what we want to achieve. We want to greet the horse (say hello), so we take a step or two towards the animal and then back up a step or two. By backing away a step, we actually are showing respect and asking permission to approach the horse for more greeting. Simply walking up to the horse and touching it is disrespectful and can scare a horse. The horse will generally look at us when we back away and may even turn towards us a bit. This is the horse's acknowledgement and gratitude for our respect, as well as it showing interest in us.

Next, we might slowly and thoughtfully approach the animal's neck or shoulder, keeping our hands down. Again, this is a respectful way of beginning this conversation. If the animal moves away from us, we should back up a step to assist the horse in understanding we mean it no harm. Compare this to a typical conversation between any two people you may see on the street. The conversation is very animated with much gesturing and waving of the hands. The speech is often loud, rapid and one person does not hesitate to speak over the other. To us, this is normal. It is definitely not normal for a horse.

Some people call me a horse whisperer. I think I am just a good conversationalist for a horse. I speak calmly, quietly, precisely, thoughtfully, clearly and respectfully. I understand the animal's body language quite well and can respond appropriately. I never make demands. I do make requests. Actually, I prefer to suggest things to a horse rather than try to tell it what to do. Through suggestions, the horse actually begins to figure out for itself what it is I am trying to communicate. This is always best. Having a successful conversation with a horse means that information and feelings have been exchanged in a positive way. Feelings of safety and trust have been preserved and perhaps even brought to a higher level.

Having a conversation with a horse is not about talking nonsense. Likewise, it is obviously not talking about world politics or the like. But it is an honest sharing of feelings, desires and intentions. Some folks say horses think in pictures. I tend to agree with this. It should be obvious to us all that they do, in fact, think in some form or another. If we accept they think in pictures and that horses are emotional animals (feeling a range of emotions from fear to elation), then the pictures in a horse's mind have an emotional attachment. The pictures either feel good or they do not. If we think about it, our thoughts have emotional content and feelings attached to them as well – they can either prompt us to feel good or not. This is why many motivational speakers tell us that if we are having thoughts that do not support us in feeling good, we can choose to change our minds – our minds being the only thing we really can choose to change in this life.

With this essay I wish to suggest we can all be better conversationalists with our horses, and in doing this we will become more successful with them. A conversation does not have to be long to be good. It does not have to be particularly "deep" as to subject or topic to be successful. It does, however, have to leave both parties feeling good. Then they will probably be very happy to come back together for more.

8 Gaining Confidence with Horses

This is a big issue for people beginning their lives with horses and some who have been with horses 'forever' but never really learned anything about their real nature. It is easy to be afraid of horses if we know nothing about them. The subject of 'confidence' is just as big for the horse as for the human (both need to have confidence). Confidence for the horse translates to 'trust'. The horse is always asking whoever is around it; "Can I trust you? Do you know what to do to help me to feel safe? Can I have confidence that I am safe if you lead me? Can I have confidence if I do as you request that I will not be hurt and will continue to be safe?" The horse has to have confidence in whoever is leading it, be they horse or human. If it does not have confidence it will be safe, the horse will instinctively begin to fend and look out for itself.

For the human, confidence with a horse means having the knowledge that you know what to do in most all circumstances that will help the horse to trust and be confident it is safe. Developing this confidence is something that really does take place over time. There is no magic pill you can take that will give you the knowledge and confidence that experience over time will. However, there are a few things people can do that will accelerate their development, learning and confidence with horses. One of these things is to read books, look at videos and attend seminars on the topic of horse training (not riding) as much as possible. Forget about becoming a great rider for now and focus on the horse itself. If a ' gentle horse trainer' (not a riding instructor) is in your area, call them and see if its possible to spend some time with them watching what they do. Being able to see the process is a huge help in acquiring the knowledge that is desirable. Videos are also great for that. Most horse magazines have numerous videos advertised in them. So, the first thing I would suggest is for interested people to find learning aids that can be viewed and trainers to watch.

Being "patient" with the horse is extremely important. If one can really develop 'great patience' in the face of a confused, fearful horse, they will gain immediate confidence in their ability to stay with the process of bringing the horse back to feelings of safety, whatever that process is. Patience just by itself is a huge plus in anyone's life. If you can stay calm and understand the goal and overall agenda of the horse's sense of safety as being paramount and patiently work towards that always, your confidence will be increased right away.

Learning to move appropriately around a horse is not that hard but very important. First of all, always be thoughtful and respect the horse's personal space. The horse will tell you by its demeanor, its posture, movements and attitude if it is comfortable with someone entering its personal space. Not unlike a human having an appropriate boundary, the horse needs you to respect its boundaries. Most people do not respect the horses right to personal space and invade the animal's boundaries constantly (reaching into a horse's face to pet its nose is a perfect example of this). Always connect first by talking to the horse before you get too close. You'll know (intuit, observe) if the horse is OK with you approaching it. If it is not, respect that and talk to it some more and move around the horse at a safe distance until the horse feels OK about you approaching it and invites you closer with its responses via body language. You'll keep yourself a lot safer too. Do not stand directly in front of the horse. Horses are by nature claustrophobic. They also want to be able to look ahead and around for possible danger. Standing by the left or right shoulder is always the safest place to stand, for the horse as well as the human. Most horses have been handled mainly on the left side, so they are most comfortable with the human standing on their left side (by the neck or shoulder). Also, you are much less likely to be bitten or kicked in that position when near a horse. Horses kick those behind them because they feel threatened or have been surprised. So, if you want to walk behind a horse talk to him, keep one hand on his rump and stay very close as you move around him so he knows where you are and your intention is simply to move around him. When grooming the tail stand a bit to the side, not directly behind the horse. There is a kick zone to avoid if possible. That zone is the place where the horse can obviously 'nail' you with a kick if it were inclined. Kicking is mostly a defense mechanism. As is any kind of seemingly aggressive behavior. The horse is protecting itself. This behavior does not deserve punishment; it deserves compassion, understanding and leadership to bring the horse back to a 'safe place' in its mind and feelings.

As far as a horse lunging or kicking at a human when bridling, that is not typical behavior. Only if the horse is made uncomfortable and, therefore, fearful by how the human is handling it trying to put the bridle on, will he either move towards the human or away. There is an appropriate way to ask a horse to accept the bridle (and saddle). It is somewhat detailed and will be addressed in another essay. If you make the horse nervous by inappropriately trying to get him to accept the bridle or saddle, it will set up a situation where he has no confidence in the human's ability to ask him to accept new things. It will get harder and harder to bridle or saddle him. Horses get habitual (take on habits) very fast and habits are hard to change. When bridling a horse, it is best to first get the horse comfortable with lowering his head when asked to. When introducing a blanket and saddle it is best to 'sack the horse out' first extensively. This means getting him used to the blanket and things flapping around and on him.

Here is a good procedure to practice for asking a horse to lower its head: with a halter (preferably a rope halter) and lead rope already on the horse, stand on the horse's left side halfway up his neck. Hold the lead rope about 18 inches under his chin and just allow the weight of your arm to come on to the rope. Do not try to pull the horse's head down. Just let the weight of your arm be there. The horse will, at some point, lower his head just a bit to get away from the weight of your arm. The instant you feel that horse lower his head, even a fraction of an inch, remove the weight of your arm completely by lifting your arm just a tiny bit up or releasing the rope. Then, do it again. You are asking the horse to lower his head by doing this. You might also bend forward with your body just a bit to encourage him to follow your body language down and look down at the ground (where you want the horse's head to go). A human should be able to get a horse to lower his head as low as requested. He'll just about put his nose on the ground if asked appropriately. A horse with a lowered head is a relaxed horse. I ask horses to lower their heads sometimes if they get a little nervous. So, it is always a good skill to have. You may want to get really good at this one as it will help you ask the horse to accept the bridle by lowering his head. It is important not to hit the horse's teeth with the bit as well. Anyway, if this procedure is practiced it will help a human gain confidence and skill. It will also help a human to understand how to begin to 'read' a horse.

'Reading' a horse means being able to ascertain what is going on for the horse in any one moment. Is the horse calm, nervous, upset, anxious, trusting, afraid, in pain or whatever? This is a very important skill to development. It will also help to develop confidence, even if all the proper 'moves' are not known yet. If a human can look at a horse and begin to 'feel' what is going on for it, they will have a skill that is priceless. The way to develop this skill is through patience, kindness and the desire to help the horse feel safe first and foremost, and not just grab him and use the horse for something. It means moving slowly observing the horse's responses to whatever the human does. It means not approaching too fast and connecting first. It means showing respect. It also means using intuition. Intuition and 'feel' have similar meanings when applied to horses. You intuit what a horse is feeling. We do this kind of thing all the time. When we meet someone new or go to a new place or try something new, it either feels OK or not. It can feel 'right or wrong'. Our brains (our intellect) may say something is OK to do, but our heart (or gut) says it is not. We follow our intuition when we follow our hearts. Horses have a very developed intuitive sense. They intuit if something wants to 'eat them for dinner'. They intuit if there is a predator present long before it gets close. They have to because it is their survival. I connect with horses a long ways away from them. By the time I get up to them we are connected and feeling good about each other (unless the horse has some abuse issues and is fearful of humans in general). I can intuit that quickly and respond accordingly to help the horse to know I am no threat to it. Developing our intuition will help develop our confidence.

If a horse moves into my space while being led or if I am in close quarters with it (the stall), I do not want to get physical with it to ask it to move away. Many times pushing a horse will prompt the horse to push back and they will always win a test of strength. Rather I have gotten very good at shaking (snaking) the lead rope under the horse's chin which is annoying to the horse and will prompt the horse to move away from the shaking rope. I will also face the horse, shake the rope and move towards the horse confidently asking it to back a step or two. This will generally allow a human to begin to set a boundary with the horse as to how close the horse can be. If there is no lead rope and halter on the horse, such as in the stall, I will wave my hand quickly right under the horse's chin or at his nose. This will generally get him to lift his head and take a step away. I have developed a 'feel' for what is too much pressure or energy in the shaking or waving so as to not scare the horse. I can also appropriately shake a rope or a wand at the horse as well (or my glove). It is important to be able to set a boundary with a horse. This one skill alone will bring tremendous confidence, as the human will understand how to get their boundaries respected. Setting appropriate boundaries is a good life skill to have. Success with horses is a great way develop skills that enrich us in all areas of our lives.

A Natural Way to Improved Mental Health, Successful Relationships and Balance in One's Life.

Horses are like magnets for humans. People of all ages are drawn to the horse because of their beauty, grace, power, majestic stature and the mystery of their noble being. It's been that way throughout recorded history. In modern times, it has been clinically documented that just being around horses changes the brain wave patterns of humans, lowers blood pressure and reduces stress. We calm down and become more centered and focused in the present moment when we are around horses. We are transformed in a very positive way when in the presence of horses. It is no wonder that the beneficial effects of positive and appropriate interaction with horses should prove therapeutic to grownups and children alike.

I first discovered Equine Facilitated Learning over 30 years ago when I began researching, via the Internet, various ways people were interacting with horses. The North America Riding for the Handicapped Association (NARHA now called PATH), a non-profit, national organization here in the United States, had a new program called the Equine Facilitated Mental Health Association (EFMHA). These particular programs sought to focus help not so much for individuals with physical challenges, but rather centered on the emotional and mental health development of children and adults when they were put in the company of horses and guided appropriately through positive interaction. Startling improvement was observed in children with various mental and emotional challenges from A.D.D. to Autism, to anti-social violent behavior. Great improvement was seen 'across the board'. This interested me a lot as I have always believed that horses can produce positive mental and emotional effects within the humans around them if the interaction was appropriate. So, I visited several places offering training in this new field and took their courses.

Upon returning to my ranch on Maui I began The Maui Horse Whisperer Experience, which was an experiential, interactive, hands-on experience of horses for non-horse people (experienced horse people and horse owners were invited as well). The positive effects of this type of successful inter-species communication were immediate and, sometimes, life altering. The confidence and self-esteem of individuals who were able to bond and communicate with the horses dramatically improved and the improvement was immediate. People would drop their projections, misconceptions and judgments about the horse and themselves once the communication became conscious, mutual and appropriate.

For children with mental and emotional disorders the positive benefits of the experience with the horses was frequently profound. Children with Attention Deficit Disorder would magically focus on the horse for long periods of time when either grooming or leading the horses. Once they understood how to ask for and receive cooperation from the horse, their self-esteem went sky high. What a wonderful sight it is when I see a shy, withdrawn, fearful child standing tall and confident as they lead a 1200-pound animal through an obstacle course of a series of twists, turns and stops. Children with Autism who would come to me mostly withdrawn and very much in their own world, would begin to say new words and attempt to express themselves as rarely seen by their parents and therapists. Given the lead rope of a horse they would proudly lead the horse around the ranch for extended periods of time and not want to give them up. Observers would stand there with mouths a gasp and tears streaming down their faces to see such profound and wonderful response in their children and wards. Once again, the horse is easily recognized as a positive force and influence for humans.

Equine Facilitated Learning is gaining popularity across this country and around the world. Prisons have instituted similar programs to assist in the rehabilitation of inmates. Wild horses are given over to some prisons so the prisoners can train and gentle them to get them ready to be adopted out. Techniques are shown the prisoners on how to gently communicate with a fearful horse and develop the trust needed to help the horse accept human contact and interaction. The inmates discover that respect, gentleness, mindfulness, compassion and kindness go a lot farther than brutality, dominance and force. These programs are so successful as to have become the single most effective form of rehabilitation for the penal system today.

At about the same time The Maui Horse Whisperer Experience came about, I began 'Leading With Quiet Strength'. This is a leadership/teambuilding program developed for corporations seeking to advance the leadership qualities and skills of top executives. There are now a few programs across the country that focuses on these goals for the corporate world utilizing guided, successful interaction with horses. In this age of corporate greed, poor management, distrust, and wide spread fraud, a program that teaches responsibility, accountability, respect, trust and mindful interaction was a natural development for Equine Facilitated Learning. My current list of clients includes; AT&T Wireless, GM, Charles Schwab & Associates, Murtiz Group and others. Enlightened leadership is a goal being pursued by many top organizations around the world. Accountability and responsibility are taught through interaction with horses and the feedback is immediate. Success or failure of the interaction and communication is tossed back into the face of the human right away in the response of the horse. If there is a problem, it can be quickly recognized and corrected by the human. Once everything is back on track, the interaction again becomes successful. A horse forgives us our mistakes. If a horse is abused by a human and eventually the human changes their way of dealing with the horse, the horse will forgive the human their mistakes and accept the friendship if it is offered appropriately.

The principles of Equine Facilitated Learning are basic and easy to understand. The horse is the perfect mirror of the human that is with it (horses do not lie). The horse is looking to have feelings of safety and peace always. This is because the horse is a 'prey' animal always looking over its shoulder for the 'predator'. If the human is trying to control the animal for whatever reason, this produces fear within the horse. If the human is unconscious around the horse, this makes the horse fearful as well. If the human is disrespectful of the horse (inappropriate touching, movements, sounds, thoughts or feelings), this produces fear with the horse too. When the human begins to make conscious and appropriate requests, rather than demands, of the horse cooperation begins to happen. When a human waits for and notices responses of the horse to the human's communication that is showing acknowledgement and respect for the horse. Trust and respect are earned with horses in much the same way as with people. The 'golden rule' applies to horses. However, with the added aspect of great guidance and leadership coming forward from the human. It is the human's responsibility to approach the horse as a great parent approaches a child. Along with the love, compassion, patience and consistency of a great parent, comes confident, skillful, knowledgeable guidance and leadership. In the wild the horse gets its sense of peace and safety from the herd leader. Unfortunately for the domesticated horse, there usually is no great human leader filling that role of the herd leader. Relationships between domesticated horses can be somewhat different, as stables and barns are an unnatural environment for horses. There are no humans making appropriate requests that the horse can follow and comply with. Horses miss this good leadership. What normally is the case are humans making unconscious, inappropriate demands, trying to control this big beast through dominance, punishment and restraint and abusing the animal through ignorance and misconception. Compliance is frequently done through bribing with food or inducing fear. A child, even one with mental or emotional disorders, given a little insight into joining appropriately with a horse, becomes the natural leader the horse is looking for. Peace abounds and cooperation and compliance come forth from the horse when the communication from the human is kind and appropriate. Actually, children can become successful with a horse quicker and easier than with many adults. This is because children are frequently less judgmental and more open to 'heart to heart' forms of communication than adults who seek 'to control' all much of the time.

Simple, clear, conscious requests are what the horse is looking for. Stop, go, backup and turn this way or that, are examples of simple requests that a human can make of a horse, clearly and consciously. When the horse complies, a thank you in the form of a "Good Boy" is all that is needed. Horses understand acknowledgement. They know that they are being respected and acknowledged when praise is offered. I am not talking about fawning over a horse because it is compliant. Overdone praise becomes shallow and meaningless. A simple "Good Boy (or Girl)" is all that is required. There is a balance to be struck. We humans seem to have a tendency to either over do or under do something. Being out of balance has become our way of being in the world. There is a natural balance to a horse's being. There is to ours as well but we do not see or feel it because of our need to 'control'. This puts us out of balance a lot in our lives. We are either too much or too little. Or, at least it seems that way. Appropriate, successful interaction with horses can lead us back to that natural balance because to be successful with a horse that balance has to be present in the communication. Equine Facilitated Learning supports natural balance coming forward in all those participating. A natural balance begins to appear when there is consideration, thoughtfulness, awareness and kindness present in the interaction. 'Balance' is another great lesson and attribute taught by Equine Facilitated Learning.

When I teach the gentle horse training techniques through my 'Way of the Horse/Training Thru Trust' seminars I am constantly using Equine Facilitated Learning.

Children coming to me for emotional or mental health development experience this Equine Facilitated Learning too. CEO's coming for leadership/teambuilding improvement, experience Equine Facilitated Learning as well. The benefits of this type of simple, yet successful interaction with horses, is immediate, profound and wide reaching. It is part of my personal mission to bring Equine Facilitated Learning to other parts of the world to benefit as many people (and horses) as possible.

10 "We Hold These Truths to be Self-Evident..."

This above quote from the United States Declaration of Independence is the beginning of one of the best-known sentences in the English language. The sentence speaks of freedoms and equality amongst men. As I watched the movie *Lincoln* recently and heard these words yet again, I was struck by the fact that what is stated is logically, morally and undeniably true. To think otherwise just didn't make any sense to me. How could buying, selling and possessing human beings as slaves be an acceptable way of life for so many, for so long is beyond me. Additionally, a truth that is self-evident, I feel, is a powerful truth. But what does this have to do with horses?

Over the many years I have been fortunately and closely associated with horses, I hear humans constantly judging the animal as bad, stubborn, naughty and deliberately disobeying their human masters. It saddens me greatly that there is so much misunderstanding of such a wonderful creature as the horse. It is judged so unfairly by humans who actually have limited experience with them, yet think they are experts. Additionally, some people who have owned horses and ridden most of their lives can do the same thing. Even certified riding instructors can inappropriately blame and label a horse as being bad and naughty. Horses do not think as humans do (thankfully). They react to their environment either with fear, because it is a prey animal, eaten by predators, or trust that they will be safe and survive because of the smart, experienced and wonderful leadership provided by their herd leader(s). For me, a self-evident truth is that the horse is always innocent, no matter what. I believe this is such an obvious truth that I cannot think otherwise. It is an animal and does not have the self-serving ego of a human. Its main goal is feelings of safety and that it will survive. A wild horse's survival is dependent upon it following its leader and cooperating with that leader in all ways. When humans become the good leader for the horse, the same will happen.

Most all behavioral problems with horses, other than pain related issues, stem from a lack of leadership based on trust. For horses and human, trust equals feelings of safety and trust is always earned through mutually successful experiences over time. From my years with horses, I have also learned that trust and respect, with a horse, are earned and arrive together. If a horse trusts you, it will respect you and vice versa. They trust and respect their leader in the wild. They may from time to time offer a challenge to her leadership. This is simply to ask if that horse is still able and willing to be the leader. One day it will not because it is too old or infirm and another horse will need to take her place. So, an occasional challenge is to be expected from a horse and not to be taken that the animal is being bad. A competent horse person should be able to recognize this bit of resistance for what it is and deal appropriately with it. It does not require punishment. The good leader will deal with it as effectively and efficiently as possible and then move on.

The good leader will answer the challenge without malice, anger or resentment. Often it is only a matter of resetting a boundary that will do the job. This works for the equine or human leader of the horse herd. Setting and keeping spatial boundaries quickly earns the respect and trust of a horse.

Directing all movement (each and every start, direction, speed and stop) and setting boundaries with horses are probably the easiest and quickest ways to begin to develop trust, respect and partnership with a horse. Asking a horse to maintain a 2-foot personal space boundary around the human is a wonderful exercise. Being able to direct all movement also establishes who the true leader is. Repeatedly asking for one, two or three steps-at-a-time and stop will get the horse's attention on the human. The stop is actually the reward in this case. The best reward for any horse is total removal of pressure and a complete stop serves that purpose very well. Stop, take a few moments and breathe and then repeat the exercise. Additionally, when providing this exercise, it is important the human not allow the horse the distraction of any eating (grass or otherwise). This process, consciously and properly executed for only 5 minutes, most often will provide amazing results. It will keep the horse's attention on the human as the leader of all movement and the reward will develop trust. Over time the complexity of the requests can increase and good effort will be continuously offered by the horse.

This same process works quite well for riding horses and for horses at the beginning of training. Even experienced, well-trained horses will benefit from a one-step-at-a-time exercise offered occasionally as something different for the horse to do and think about. A rider should initially ask for something small like only a few steps in an arc and then stop (whoa) and breathe. Repeating this exercise will do the same thing for a rider as it did for the leader on the ground. Of course, a nervous or high-strung horse may not be able to relax enough to take smaller steps and will resist this. In this case no restraint should be applied, but rather directed movement is the best response by the human. Lead and guide where the horse goes. Generally, this will be in a circle if the horse is on a line or around an arena, paddock or round pen if the animal is at liberty. If the horse is being ridden is anxious and fearful, guided movement is always the best. As all movement is work for a horse, it will not want to move forever and the human leader needs to be able to hang in there until the nervous energy is removed via this directed movement (work). Trotting is a terrific gate and exercise for an anxious horse. A nervous, agitated horse cannot pay attention to anything. Calm and then focus must be restored before any learning can be accomplished by a horse.

Additionally, acceptance that a horse is always innocent helps us to be calmer and more focused when with our horses. We will give up anger towards the horse and resentment no matter what the behavior. Probably all frustration will diminish as well. I have always found value in developing my own inner peacefulness. I have no doubts that this has assisted me to be more successful in my relationships with horses (and humans too). I discovered a long time ago that horses are attracted to a peaceful place. I always want being with me to be that peaceful place for the horses I am with. It can work miracles in our interactions and success with horses and each other. Keep in mind to give the gift of peace we have to find it within ourselves first as we cannot give what we do not have. I always suggest we seek to develop our own inner peacefulness as much as possible. I think developing our inner peace is a journey, as is life. It is not a destination but rather a path we can choose to walk. If we chose the path of peace we may find our horses happily and willingly walking by our side and with us all the way.

11 Quick Quote Reminders

A horse will fend for itself and become its own leader in the absence of another good, trusted leader being with it. This "fending for itself" behavior can be aggressive and dangerous. But it is still based in the fear of not surviving. When horses are made to be afraid over even a brief period of time, this fear becomes habitual feelings for the horse and the behavior accompanying it becomes habitual as well.

Ten things you can do for your horse: First offer compassion and kindness, second acquire wisdom and knowledge, third provide excellent and clear communication, fourth show respect and thoughtfulness, fifth be trustworthy and have integrity, sixth offer consistent support for feelings of safety and trust, seventh learn to reward effort with peace, eighth have partnership be a goal, ninth never get angry at the horse, tenth never make it afraid. These things would help a lot...

Many problems with horses could be resolved quickly by the human asking for some small, simple movement as soon as they get with/near their horse. Step back, step forward, stop, and reward by the human stepping back. Doing this even before you go into the stall (from the outside), will quickly establish who is the leader of today's dance. This will also reinforce your connection and your boundaries. Be the good leader. Your horse will love you even more.

Wishing and hoping are fine. But real accomplishment and successes mostly happen from long hours of practice, acquiring knowledge and lots of hard work. You are blessed if you love what you do so much that you are happy to put your heart and soul into it, for however long it takes. Enjoy the ride......

Keep it simple. Keep it fun. Reward all effort. Ask for one-step-at-a-time (less is more with horses). Respect boundaries and keep your own intact. Offer wonderful leadership along with clear and precise communication. Be compassionate and kind. Now go out and have a terrific day!

In learning to 'read' a horse, it is extremely important that we pay attention to our intuitive and instinctive voices. Attempting to figure the horse out takes too long and most often will lead us away from what is really going on. Feeling the situation out is a far better way to assess the possibility of danger or harm to us or the horse. The voices of instinct and intuition can be easier heard through practice. Riding instructors should be teaching this along with riding skills. I have rarely heard of an instructor teaching a student how to 'read' a horse. Stand still, be quiet, breath and feel...

Rather than trying to figure out what may be wrong in your relationship with your horse (or others) and why you are having this or that problem, consider what works well and build on that. If you go in a positive direction the chances of success are improved greatly.

Wonderful teaching provides the student with the 'why' as well as the 'what.'

Unfortunately, the development of trust with horses is rarely even thought of as the primary and most important ingredient in having a safe, compliant and confident horse. Most training is about wanting a horse to perform a specific task. Trust is rarely thought of as the main component in successful training.

We humans often only show up as the caretaker and boss for our horses. When the boss speaks, it is mostly a one- sided conversation. Not being 'heard' within a conversation goes along with not being respected or even acknowledged that we are there. This is how it often is for the horse.

The primary, motivating, and inspirational part of a relationship with a horse is what is in my heart. Remembering that what I say is secondary to what I demonstrate through being as present as I can, as authentic as I can, and holding a compassionate and loving outlook towards the horse. This can help all relationships I think.

How many times can your trust be betrayed before you get out of a relationship? Therefore it should be easy to understand how, even one time, ignoring the best interests of your horse, will prompt distrust, disrespect and behavior you really rather not have. Consider your horse first.

Consider avoiding expectations and assumptions with horses. If you do this with your partner, children or others, you are setting yourself up for disappointment. Avoiding assumptions and expectations opens us to possibilities of even greater happenings than we would have expected or assumed. Things don't always work out as we would have preferred. But avoiding projections brings with it the possibilities of receiving greater gifts then we thought possible. This really works great with horses. NOW is the great present of life.

This is going to be a very difficult concept for most all to accept. But I really want to suggest you think about this and, if you really understand the horse, I think you will see it is the truth. "There are no stubborn or resistant horses. There are only stubborn and resistant trainers and riders."

The collapse of the ego as superior is dramatic, profound, humbling and develops an opened heart, the ability to offer unselfish love and opens avenues towards a more fulfilling and happier life.

To have a life with horses is to have a life directed towards peace. It is not about winning and getting awards. It is about giving and offering kindness, compassion, peace and love. It is more about "being" than "doing." Any things beyond these are extra gifts and to be received with gratitude and humility.

I never liked being told what to do. Neither do horses. Suggesting something to me, if I felt it reasonable and worthwhile, usually brought a good response. It is the same with horses. If a horse has accepted us as its good/trusted leader, generally we get a good response from 'suggesting' or 'asking' for what we want. I admit I get 'triggered' when someone says I "must" do or be this or that to achieve something. Precisely suggesting or clearly and gently asking something works quite well with horses, me and is an indication of a good leader.

With horses it does not matter how fast the horse can do something (unless running a race). Trying to train a horse that is moving fast is impossible. In order to learn, the horse must be calm. In order to teach the horse anything, we must be calm and focused as well. It does not often matter how fast we can do something. What does matter is how well we can do it. If we can train a horse to do something slowly that is terrific as we can always speed him up once he learns it. Slow, steady and precise is the way to go...Breath!!!

Don't be so attached to a particular trainer's method or even your own tried and true techniques. The ability to be creative and spontaneous make for even more possibilities for success as far as horse training goes. Every horse is different. What has worked for you with all the horses in the past may not work for the next one. Be flexible and kind always. Works with people too......

We learn from a horse through paying close attention to its responses to everything we do when near it. It will respond to things we do not even realize we are doing. It will respond to things we do not see or hear. By paying attention to our horse's communications through its responses and actions when near us, we can then modify what we are doing to make successful communication more of a possibility.

I think dealing with our fears is a life-long process. As I age and see the slew of talented younger horsemen and women coming up, I can wonder if there is still a place for me. When I was younger and saw the many talented clinicians out there with bigger advertising budgets, slicker promotions and awards from competitions, I would wonder if I was good enough. I am not a competitive person. I chose to focus on horses more than competitions with them. After all these years I can still have doubt. But when I just follow my heart and listen to my intuition, somehow things continue to work out. Not to worry...

If you are going with your horse today, consider slowing everything down. If you can ask (train) your horse to do things in slow motion and precisely, you will have no trouble speeding things up when ready. Consider one-step-at-a-time and reward (removal of pressure and total peace) as an effective and positive reinforcement system of training. Build on small successes and they will become big ones eventually. Notice all reactions and responses of your horse as this is the animal trying to communicate with you. You do not need to be Buck B. (and he is very good) to do this stuff. You need strong desire, commitment, compassion, knowledge of horses and a lot of patience.

More than control, dominance, being a boss, or master, or being in charge, patience, compassion, wisdom, skill and trust will lead you and your horse to success

THE FUTURE

12 Letters

So, my quest for better information to help my horse Lucky has led me to you! I am going to try to read more of what you have to say and put it into practice. When I read your book, I felt like I had finally found another person who understands what Lucky has been trying to teach me...And that I am not crazy, and that this horse is not deliberately trying to defy me. There are not many trainers or horse people in general who really understand that. That is why we need you. I am so glad to read your writings...I feel like Helen Keller must have felt when someone was finally able to get through to her, and teach her to read and communicate, even though she was blind! You will be able to help me communicate with this horse that I love, but who speaks an entirely different language than me!

Holly, Arizona

I finished reading your book and I am completely mesmerized and at a total loss for words. There are not enough superlatives! You must truly be at one with the horses you train. EVERY horse owner should read, study, and put into practice your brilliant book.

Thank you for sharing it with me.
God Bless
Jack Hofstra , A.C.E.

Franklin, your eBook is a stellar piece of work. Well done my friend- I have read and reread it multiple times. I notice when I read it my breathing changes, my heart feels content and I have an overall sense of well-being. You not only delivered incredibly helpful information, but you have constructed your thoughts in such a manner it feels meditative to the reader. I hope it translates to all in their lives and their work with horses. You are a gift to the Universe and a blessing to all. We love you both dearly and appreciate your kindness in sharing beyond measure.

With love always ~ Andy

A fantastic book by Franklin Levinson I loved reading this and the story of Sweet Pete who was so misunderstood. We have a lot to learn in how we work with our horses and I would recommend this to everybody who owns a horse.

Amanda, Scotland

It was about time to make this move, this book...!! I am so proud of you! You know how it felt to me? Not like reading an ordinary book... but as if you are trying to pass your inheritance/legacy, as if you are not only sharing knowledge and experience, but actually establishing a true and permanent connection with all of us who seek for inspiration and motivation to be and become better horsemen and women...not only by trying to understand the horse but understand the horse through you... through the way you proved it works best for both horses and people. It is so... "Franklin" and that's what makes the difference into it. Passing on not just words and techniques but actual and true wisdom. I think that is what most horsemen lack wisdom. That's what it feels like to me and I love it! Please consider translating it into Greek too!!!

Love, K, Greece

Franklin Levinson is like a brother to me. I have known him for close to 20 years, worked with him, played with him, laughed with him, cried with him. Now I celebrate with Franklin and rejoice with all of the people and horses he shall touch through this book. It is truly an art to reach the heart of the reader in a manner that also offers guidance and practical approaches to common challenges, be they in life or with a horse. In *Trust 'n Horses*, Franklin brings his lifetime of experience with horses to all of us, and we are the better for it. Perhaps more importantly, so are our horses.

Dr. Lee Jampolsky, Best-Selling Author.
www.drleejampolsky.com

I just finished *Trust 'n Horses*. Fabulous info and a great beginning and reminder for any horseman or woman. If horsemen took this piece seriously, really absorbed it, just think how much LESS misunderstanding and abuse would take place. The reference to Francis of Assisi, your dysfunctional upbringing, etc. all speaks to me. I do believe those of us from such situations actually have an edge as we feel empathy at a level so many don't. This is an excellent read and recommended for horsemen and women of every skill level.

Frank Bell
www.horsewhisperer.com

Am really enjoying your e-book Franklin Levinson - found the chapter about building trust especially informative and touching...

Thank You! Carolyn Seager

Thank you for creating this book *Trust 'n Horses*! I especially loved reading about Sweet Pete, your affection for him reads loud and clear in your words, it's rather beautiful! I really appreciated that the book is about understanding the horse(s) and understanding the nature of the horse to better understand your nature with the horse. You are always saying start with the basics and I believe this book is a bible for those who want to do so. Start with the most vital yet often over looked element of horse training, the horse. I always enjoy reading, watching and listening to your words of wisdom as they inspire me to be better with my horse and everything I do. Thank you for sharing this book with me. I will recommend it to everyone! It will be my bible! After all Everyone needs something to believe in.

Love, Jessie

I really enjoyed reading it, Franklin. Your stories and insights. Reading this was kind of a meditation of sorts...leaving me with an overall "way" instead of a hard and fast "to do" list. I am sure I will read it many more times.

Heather Roman

Franklin Levinson and I have been the closest of friends for over 20 years and he has remained an important teacher of mine. He has helped me to let of any residual fear that a horse will necessarily hurt me. I have watched him transform the lives of children with cancer, business men and women and people from all walks of life.

He helps all who witness his teachings to be more gentle, kind, compassionate, patient with ourselves and others and that our relationship with horses can carry through to human relations and all of life. And above all, to be determined not to have thoughts, attitudes or actions that are hurtful to any others including ourselves.

May you enjoy the lessons this book will offer you.

Gerald G, Jampolsky, M.D.
Attitudinal Healing International
www.attitudinalhealinginternational.org
Co-author of "A mini Course for Life"
Love is Letting Go of Fear
Teach Only Love

Hey Franklin! I read through your entire book and loved it! Your wisdom is impeccable, your heart open, and everything you said resonated deeply. Thank you for all the experience you have gained that you are sharing with your students and readers, and for your compassion and kindness to animals. I'm sure that anyone who wishes to relate to any animal can and will benefit, and of course the animals they love. I look forward to the book getting out there and touching and inspiring lots of people.

Alan Cohen, Author
"The Dragon Doesn't Live Here Anymore"
"I Had It All the Time"

I just finished reading Franklin Levinson's new e-book *Trust 'n Horses*. I loved it! He put words on horsemanship I believe in, and he's great at it. He mixes a lifetime of experience with horses, with interesting stories (examples from his life,) that answer the question WHY? What happens if I do it this way? The title of his book, *Trust 'n Horses*, says everything about the kind of horsemanship Franklin prefers. Franklin's philosophy is for the well-being of the horse. One of the benefits doing things in a way the horse can understand it's a beautiful relationship, a wonderful experience with your horse. It's definitely the safest way of spending time with a horse as well.

Franklin collects a lifetime of wisdom, into an easy to read eBook. It covers many different aspects in our life with horses, from scratch (building a long-lasting relationship); from *Learning to be With Horses* (Chapter 2), to (Chapter 5) *Five Tips for Getting That New Horse to Love You*. The horse stories he includes in the book touches one's heart and shows that there's hope for any horse/human relationship – if we're open to learn how to speak Equus. Communicate in a way the horse can understand and create a safe place for the horse. I can highly recommend this book to everyone who would like to improve their horsemanship skills. It doesn't matter if you just started with horses, or admired them your whole life, like I have. Franklin has food for thoughts, on all levels.

One of the things that fascinate me personally with horses is that I realize how much I have to learn, on a daily basis. I haven't had any other passion that lasted since I was 2-years old. Have you? For me it's probably because there's always room for improvements. Before I get too old, I would like to see exactly how far I can take a relationship with a horse. I would like to see how well I can refine my communication, with one specific horse. And what kind of possibilities that relationship would open up. This is not something that I'm planning to make a lot of money doing. I would like to learn more for myself, and for the sake of the horses I meet.

Maria Northcutt

I have read Franklin's *Trust 'n Horses*, volumes one and two. I think he has some huge missing pieces that lots of the other "natural" horse trainers miss. That is the kindness piece, and the knowledge that the horse's "bad" behavior is based in fear, not a deliberate attempt to defy the human. I think I innately knew this, but it really helped to hear it seconded from Franklin, as lots of the other trainers preach about respect, disrespect, making the horse mind you, etc. You can be kind and firm at the same time, and the horse will likely be happy to go along with you. Thanks, Franklin!

Holly Bowman Goldstein

Hello Franklin! I'm Guilherme Diniz, a writer from Brazil, working on a new novel. In there, the lead character (a sick woman) haves a horse, named Nimrod, and the relationship between the two is an important part of the plot. So, I, that doesn't know absolutely nothing about horses, began an internet search for good articles and sites, to understand these animals and then be able to depict them in the best form possible on my work. And then, I stumbled on you site. And I have to say, your essays are simply amazing. Your every word transpires love and understanding about these beautiful animals. Your teachings about love and respect, especially trust, are fantastic, and can be applied not only in relationships with horses but with humans as well. Your words about unconditional love, about trust being something that need to be gained over time, and so much other subjects, are powerful and inspiring.

So, I decided to use my rudimentary English (please forgive my mistakes. English is not my native language) to write this message to you, to, first, thank you. On your site I have learned not only about horses, but about life itself, and this have changed my novel in really deep level. Now, understanding horses a bit better, I can create a much more powerful relationship between Gwendolyn and Nimrod. And more, I have dedicated a large portion of the text to explain to my readers the nature of horses, based on your deep knowledge about them.

And, I, in a form to display my thanks and respect about you, gave the name "Franklin" to the man that taught all about horses to the female lead character Gwendolyn. Because you have! Not only for her, you taught everything about horses to me!

I don't know if this message will be read, but I wrote it anyway. Today you have my deepest thanks and respect, and I imagine you being a great leader and sensitive man. And I connect with that, being a sensitive man myself. In the last days I have lost my fear of riding horses. Believe or not, I live on a city where these animals are abundant, called "Barretos", a place with a rich history on rodeos and the such, and, because of my fear, I haven't approached a horse before, always admiring then only in distance. Now, I will change that, thanks to you.

So, god bless you, and, again, Thanks. My work and my life are much more rich now, with your help.

Guilherme Diniz

When a human waits for and notices the responses of the horse to the human's communications, that is showing acknowledgement and respect for the horse.   Franklin Levinson

About the Author

Franklin Levinson has been a professional horseman for nearly 50 years. At 13 years of age he was the youngest registered polo player in the US. In his early 20s he created and ran equestrian programs at large summer camps in North Michigan. He has always taught success with horses to be a life enriching process for both horse and human and that horses are never naughty or bad. In his teaching he states, "All unwanted behavior from a horse is a symptom of the animal's fear and never deserves punishment." He is adamant about humans not merely 'using' horses for selfish enjoyment. Franklin's goal that the horse and human become partners through the inspired and excellent leadership of the human. Additionally, his desire is that the horse be honored and highly respected within any horse – human activity. He was an outfitter and wilderness guide at his ranch on the island of Maui for 30 years (Adventures on Horseback), along the way creating The Maui Horse Whisperer experience. This was the first Equine Facilitated Learning (EFL) program in the Pacific basin and one of the first in the US. He is credited in *Your Horse Magazine* 2004, UK's premier equine magazine, as being the first person to introduce EFL for children with a learning disability to the United Kingdom. Additionally, about that same time, he is credited as the first person to bring EFL to Australia. He founded the Australia Equine Facilitated Learning Pty. Ltd. (AEFL) several years ago. With his *Training Through Trust* DVD, filmed in 2005, he created the first video documentation of EFL for children with learning disabilities. For many years, before the Natural Horsemanship bandwagon and craze, he taught his brand of gentle, effective horsemanship (*Beyond Natural Horsemanship, Successful Training through Compassion, Wisdom, Skill and Trust*) and EFL in seven countries annually. For over 25 years Franklin has been published internationally in various print media outlets. Other media credits include: podcasts, webinars and numerous television and radio appearances, on the topics of horse training, horsemanship and Equine Facilitated Learning. He even acted in a western movie titled *September Dawn* starring Jon Voight. For additional information about Franklin, including media, publications, and DVDs, visit his website www.TrustnHorses.com.

www.MauiHorses.com
www.FranklinLevinson.com
www.WayoftheHorse.org
www.MauiHorseWhisperer.com
www.ACourseinHorse.com
www.TrustnHorses.com

www.ingramcontent.com/pod-product-compliance
Lightning Source LLC
LaVergne TN
LVHW021510080426
835509LV00018B/2466